eyes speak louder than words

a collection of poems + letters

tatiana cole

EYES SPEAK LOUDER THAN WORDS: A COLLECTION OF POEMS
AND LETTERS

Copyright © 2020 by Tatiana Cole

Published by Tatiana Cole
Brooklyn, NY

peaceofcole.com

Cover Art by Tatiana Cole
Editing by Tatiana Cole

First Printing, 2020

ISBN: 978-0-578-74642-5

ACKNOWLEDGEMENTS

Sending gratitude to my family and friends who have supported me through this journey of publishing my first book. Thank you for lending your eyes, ears, minds, and hearts.

A special thanks to my Mom, Dad, Nadia, Marcellus, and Titus. In my weakness, I find strength in you. Thank you for brightening my world each and every day.

I love you.

Tatiana

PREFACE

Thank you for purchasing my premiere book: Eyes Speak Louder than Words. I am thrilled that you've chosen to join me on this journey as I travel to and from love and every emotion in between. As much as I could have held on to this piece of literature longer it was time to finally free it so that my mind can focus on other ideas and unrealized dreams.

This book encapsulates the sum of my many moments of solitude over the past 3 years. In 2017, I resumed writing poetry and simultaneously resumed a much-needed journey into self-exploration, imaginative thinking, and reflection. I dove deep back into my love of language. At the root of that love of language is my love for what it can do. Far too often, we fail to use language when it matters most. So here is my ask to you: Today, use language in a way that serves you and others. Say what is on your heart to whom is on your mind. Every day is not promised. *Make the most of these moments, as the moments make up the life.*

I hope that this book which has found its way from my heart into your hands moves you. If it does, please share your favorite pieces with me by screenshotting and tagging me on social media at @peaceofcole. I am looking forward to reimagining my words through your lens.

I am immensely excited to share this body of work with you. If nothing else, I hope that it inspires you to live a little and feel a lot.

Love,

Tatiana

eyes speak louder than words

Phases

journey to (+ from) love

Desirous

Something magical happens
Within the distance between our lips
When they're dangling a breath away from an embrace
What sweet energy lies between them
I'll never be able to describe
It's a yearning
For the pressure of your lips on mine
It's a calling
For our tongues to dance as they always do
In the midst of that silent, breathless moment
I love to love the anticipation

Not For Keeps

Like fattened rose petals swelled with water on a rainy spring day -
I am lush.
Inhale my aroma and you too will thicken with the softness cradled within my
core.
Absorb me slowly, thoughtfully.
Enjoy me intentionally – because this moment will soon escape you.
The essence of me is not for keeps.
But the joy + pain of my release will be forever ingrained in your energy
Forever changed, you'll be-
Marked by the complexities of crossing paths with a storm of a woman like me

Erasure

Thoughts of us turn my eyes into saltwater captives
The only way to free them is to flush out your memory

icriedyourweightintears

Love Talk

When you fall in love again, read this letter.
Be kind
Be patient
Be flexible
Be support
Be a shoulder
Be a rock
Be understanding
Be innerstanding
Be fragile
Be human
Be forgiving
Be love
Be light
Be a friend
Be a lover
Be extremely patient
Be extremely flexible
Be the reason he knows love
Be the reason he knows light
Be a beautiful summer storm when life calls you to be
And just like summer storms...let your energy be the rainbow that beams after
Like healing oils, gloss over his wounds, your wounds, nurse him as he nurses
you
Be growth
Be strength
For him
But mostly, for you.

Silk

We had a love like SILK
Smooth to the touch
But jagged when cut with force

Cruel Rivers

Like a river of water in my hands, we kept slipping through my fingertips
My palms too narrow a landing space and too shallow a home
I could not catch us
Aren't rivers cruel?
Clear for us to see, but not to hold
Tangible but not to be taken captive
And dances as they escape
Unlike an ocean that sits from time to time,
A river is always on the run – but from what?
Aren't we the river too?
Weren't we what fueled its migration?

Or were we just there, slipping through the cracks while bonded together the
entire time and enjoying the ride?

Compass

I won't provide the compass to navigate my love
I know the one God sends me will yearn for this excursion
I have no interest in revising my expectations
I'm observant and I'm not into men that want the easy version
Of anything really – and I deserve a man that's willing
I'm not asking for a killing
I don't need gifts from floor to ceiling
You see – I'm more about the feeling

When we lock eyes, can I read his energy?
No time for games you can save that "is he feeling me?"
What's his aura like? Are we magnetic?
Attraction is one thing but beyond that – it can't feel synthetic

I won't provide instructions on how to be with me
I'd rather let you take the lead + I'll learn naturally if we're to be
As a woman, I come with many inclinations
Like nurturing, supporting + preserving relations
Men who won't take that for granted deserve all the praisin' - all the praisin'

Is it too much for me to want a Renaissance man?
Today's technological advances make it easier now than then
How do you spend your idle time other than on the gram?
Can you teach me something new? There's nothing like an unexpected,
"damn"

On what levels do we connect?
Don't want a clone of me – but do our interests intersect?
How do you respond to obstacles?
Are you cool, calm + collected, or completely illogical?
I won't front – I'm a firecracker myself
Something about a reserved ass brotha that screams balance + inner wealth

So, what do all of the above have to do with love?
Love is not an achievement it's anything but
It can't be crossed off on a whiteboard
And 40% effort won't make the cut
Love is a journey of endless pastures

And the grass ain't always green
And like anything else worthwhile –
Sometimes it requires swimming upstream
That's why I can't provide you a compass to navigate my love
And women who will try to will end up searching up above
Asking God why and how could he let someone soak up
All of this time and energy and leave her with an empty cup?
I won't allow someone to disguise themselves according to my instructions
Love comes without a playbook it's a natural eruption

Time Travel

Thoughts of you extract me out of the present and transports me to moments
that exploit every one of the 5 senses
I channel you in my mind, time after time after time
Until we meet again

It Takes Two

I love when you inflict our pain on me
The kind of pain we can only make together
Between my gasps for air
And your fistful of my strands
Our energy builds until it's ready to combust
My eyes are full of fire
Your chest is full of passion
Which grows with every motion
I love when I release our pain on you
The kind of pain we can only make rain down together

Ego Fight

There we go - once again we've lost track of the conversation
A brief pause presented an exit but neither one of us contemplated
Instead, we jumped in place and aligned to our respective sides
We're in battle again tonight, headed toward another ego fight
It's seldom that I remember the reason when it finally comes to a head
We forget we're on the same team and start keeping score instead
Emotional turbulence colors my mind in confusion
Time is never on our side so how we continue to abuse it?
How we continue to act like we don't know how to use it?
Egos - protected at all costs but look how we grow when we lose it?
My loved ones would never believe it but I'm willing to put mine to rest
I'm down to be the bigger person and make the most of the time that's left
That's the moment when your Taurus energy gets put to the test
But you know the synergy after our tribulations be the best
Every ill precursor stands out clear as hell in retrospect
The trials strengthen our union
Clarity clears our mind of illusions
We get away from the stressin' and start asking ourselves real questions..
Like what the fuck was we on earlier today?
Next thing you know we're back to laughing + loving in a crazy way
It reinforces that we're built to withstand whatever thang
I feel closer to you when we excuse our egos from this space
Putting our pride before our love is an everlasting disgrace
The price of pride is on the rise but ain't love a priceless thang?
For the moments it's you vs. me what's the real price that we pay?
Let's slow down, rewind + take a moment to realign
Us getting caught up in the motions is a blatant a waste of time
So please, let's stay right we don't need another ego fight

Episode 1

I often reminisce on our first love episode
No more wondering of all the ways I'd make you explode
At first sight, I knew I'd surrender to you - It was only a matter of time
I'm longing to taste our love now and be reminded of what's mine

What is Love?

I am craving a "someone"
Who will welcome with open arms
My Gratitude
My Happiness
My Humanity
My Sadness
and My Sunshine in rays

Romance

I'm not a hopeless romantic but, romance me.

Stories

How many love stories exist inside of you?
Love of sisters
Love of brothers
Love of parents
Love of grandparents
Love of aunties
Love of uncles
Love of cousins
Love of friendships
Love of lovers
Love of feelings
Love of places
Love of scents
Love of familiarity
Over the course of your life..
How many stories, love?
Thousands, I hope.

1st Exchange

Tell me what happened to your soul
When my vibrations stirred it
You wore a stern look
But your pulse never lied to me before
Now that our frames have finally met
I know that an evolution took place there
So tell me....

Immeasurable

I think about you
From the moment
The canary-colored rays
Streak out from behind the mountaintop
Hiding the true strength of its nucleus
Behind the rocky mass
Until it finds its place
In the sky

I think about you
Until the canary rays change form
Tangerine rays jet across
A pink and purple sky
God's masterpiece
Which provides us light
Always makes
A million-dollar exit
Behind the blanket of waves
Reflecting across endless beads of sand as it goes

There are two magic hours in the day
The time filled within them and between them..
Are filled with thoughts of you

Unapologetic

All the men that ever loved me
Wept the same cry
When the time came to release me
Breaking hearts were never my intention
Some did it to me….
But in the end, they always did it to themselves

Key

I crack my safety open for you like a book
But this is not physical
I invite you into the corridors of my most vulnerable spaces, revealing the
hidden faces of my past present and future loves
I sever the exterior layer of my spirit's protective film just to give you a
glimpse of the devils and angels that battle within me like they know...
Like they know that my passion for you cannot exist without both fire and ice
I peel back the layers of my soul and they crease and fold for you like they
smelled you coming
Like they smelled you deciding to come and like your arrival was all that ever
mattered to them and like their evolution depended on it
And my soul layers...
They sing songs that feel like welcome home
They know you're home before I can even warn them to thicken like roots and
hold on tight to the soil that they know because the truth is:
Your arrival changed all that I thought I knew and the further your imprint
flowers in my soul the more I find myself taking form to the pieces that fit so
intricately into our puzzle
Your existence in my world sped down like an asteroid to my earth...
Unannounced and undirected
But powerful
The blood in my veins thicken at the thought of you
You see because a single thought triggers a scent which sparks a memory
And all these pages... they're filled with memories
And could bes and should bes
And your existence permeates every sentence, paragraph, page and syllable in
my book.... My book
You crack my safety open for me like you got the cheat codes
Revealing hidden faces of my past present and future loves
You take a look - But all you see is mirrors...
All you see is mirrors and reflections of you as my past present and future
loves
I should've known
I should've known all along that you never needed a key

Eternity

Our love is an unending cyclic force
It stirred up my world the moment it landed within me
It was uninvited yet it recognized its home all along
This love was destined to be
Welcome to eternity

Silent Exchange

My eyes said all the true things to you—
But not the truths you were hoping for
Eyes speak louder than words

If Only

I'm dreaming up a world where we took things slower
A world where we allowed the curiosity between us to breathe a little longer
But we persisted.
We.
Persisted.

Misconstrued

Sometimes you send mixed signals
Like interlocked fingers
Forehead kisses
Long embraces
Reaching out just enough to not be forgotten
So much that I too have begun to send mixed signals
As a means of protection
So here we are
Two adults, not communicating how we feel
But what use is there in trying
If I can't decode the signs?

And the worst part?
Our story is not unique
Welcome, to **situationships**

Rivers Keep Rolling

Someone mentioned you to me the other day
And it reminded me that you too are still a living and breathing entity
A being that does not depend on my presence to thrive
How humbling is it to realize
That you use the same moon and sky to fuel your life's vision
And that the same sunsets that remind me of another day closed
Keep you running as well?
Every now and again, life gives me reminders of our journey to and from love
Except, these days… I feel freed from the need to shield myself from the pain
in our memories
Has the pain, then...transformed?
I know all too well how time heals
Time has been working on me
And I suppose I hadn't realized that rivers - whether in sight or not
They keep rolling

Gemini Eyes

Your eyes speak a language I've yet to learn
Your glance - a code I've yet to crack
Most men reveal their cards to me unintentionally
I read them upon their approach
Before they even fix their lips to say hello
But your eyes have depth
The kind of depth deep enough to hold secrets in plain sight
Sheltered by your cloak of mystery
My eyes speak a language you know well
But may not be ready to receive
A language of fearless truth - of vulnerability
They open to you without shields, smoke or mirrors
I hold your gaze, but not my breath
As I wait to see if you'll disarm the vessels to your soul
You blink and cut away
A subtle reminder that I won't crack your code anytime soon
Like you, your eyes say less
And instead
Allow those around you to create the narratives they want + need to believe
But not me
I tell you you're a mystery and you agree
We share a laugh
I don't admit that I'm addicted to your mystique
But you know

Cherry Starbursts (Ain't so Sweet)

I cherry-picked all of our stars from the depths of the sky
I protected your heart and left mine behind
I put in the work but fate can't be defied
This ain't sweet love, baby

Dear lover,

What is it about my thighs that drive you wild?
Their "fullness" seems to catch you by surprise
I may look light
But I'm h e a v y
And worth the weight

My Type

You're the assertive type, you know just what I need
Never second-guessing yourself when it comes to dealing with me
You know that I'm the type of woman that needs a man who's for sure
About his strengths, limitations + inspiration for more

You're never satisfied with all of the things that you know
Consistent thirst for knowledge for all of the things that you don't
Intellect by design you're an eternal student
Always assessing the consequences your movements are prudent

And shoutout to a brotha that can teach me something new
Where's the fun in a connection without a lesson or two
Our first date you had me pulling articles mid-conversation
Fact-checking our debate between the tequila we're chasing
You're opinionated like me and I respect the challenge
To acquire a new perspective I call that a check + a balance

Beyond the mental stimulants, you have other benefits
Like the way you know what, when and where deserves attention
Like the way you slowed us down + became our guide with ya lips
Like the way you know to smack it before you grip on my hips
Like the way I love the contrast of your skin next to mine
Who knew that against your chocolate frame my golden skin would shine
Like the way we didn't need to talk about it for you to understand
I'm a woman with a choice who won't be judged by a man
Based on my decision to explore your mind + your body
Understanding your perspective of the world is my new hobby

I told you I don't seek to possess ownership of my next partner
That the desire to possess another being makes keeping them harder
I talked to you about some of the lessons I've learned in love
You shared through fear you've avoided monogamy + focusing on one
You felt my thoughts on possession were revolutionary for a woman my age
You've experienced a lot of women that projected the same....
Panicked desire to mark their territory and be the one that you claim
They wanted you to climb mountaintops for the purpose of shouting their
names

Damn....
I remember when that type of woman was me
It took some hard learning + reflecting to walk to this new beat
But the new sense of self I've acquired don't require a co-signer
I know that any man that knows my worth - knows my designer
And if he can see the God in he - he will see the Goddess in me
And I will never need to force a celebration of me onto thee

I appreciate that conversation more than you know
You told me you respect me even more for doing whatever I chose
You shared you knew your opinion of me was not of any relevance
Cause when you see me you see a woman in her element who moves with elegance
There's something special about a man who doesn't feel the need to project
Any assumptions or opinions onto other subjects
Instead you move humbly with grace and a desire to understand
I appreciate a man with flexibility to bend established perceptions
Damn, I wanna connect the dots of your mind again and..
I know I pressed you out for FaceTiming me unannounced
But I love that you wanted to hear my voice + didn't block it out
So many men in our generation
Avoid their natural inclinations
For fear of getting shut down
When fear is at the root of what's tilting their crown

But you're the assertive type, you know just what I need
Never second-guessing yourself when it comes to dealing with me
You know that - I'm the type of woman that needs a man who's for sure
About his strengths, limitations + inspiration for more

Mindful Attraction

You're oblivious
To the blessing I plan to bestow on you
You'd never guess
The plans I have for us
We are hardly friends
Acquaintances at best
But I've chosen you
For a ceremony of exchange
You'll give me what I want
I'll give you what you *never knew you needed*
And what's best?
I'll leave the memory as beautiful as it is
Floating there
Without dissecting or deflecting what it means
And maybe
If we cross paths, cities, journeys once more
We'll relive this moment, together
With an intensity + familiarity greater than the time before

Appetite

You quench a bottomless appetite I never knew I had
The moment we're finished using our bodies as language...
I'm planning the ways I wanna run that back
The richness of your skin matches the richness of your mind
Black, beautiful, smooth and a compliment to mine
I can see our frames now... chocolate wrapped in gold
Ain't nothing lazy about your loving when you go in you go for my soul
And I feel it there, too
I feel blessed and stressed, too
About all of the things that you can make my body do
You're attentive to my rhythm and that's important to me
When we venture off into our world it's like we're lost at sea
Traveling with intention but not fully in control
We put our trust in the current and we roll with the flow
And ooh, don't it flow?
If that's one thing that you know
There's no lack of efficiency when you rocking with me
And when we're finished I look forward to exploring your mind
You challenge me mentally and that ain't easy to find
Wrapped in a package of a man that's so got damn fine
I look forward to each episode they're never one and the same
I'm always in for something new when I climb up on your frame
You be caressing my body while you're praising my gains

"Damn girl those workouts ain't going down in vain
Ya waist is tight
That ass looks right
And those thick thighs - they really put up a fight
And I'm up for it tonight
Ima keep you right"

And you always keep your promise you take care of me
I don't be thinking about a thing cause we're so carefree
You see - you quench a bottomless appetite I never knew I had
The moment we're finished using our bodies as language I'm planning the
ways I wanna run that back

Sparks > Fire

I remember the day you woke up and decided you didn't love anymore
And I remember questioning why I pushed you to the edge
Why I wanted you to prove your love to me so bad...
That I forced you to tumble and fall out of it
Why I decided to play with the match that would blow up my world
If only I had known, fire dancers only appear to be in control
You see, they control the mass... the ball of fire
But the sparks.... oh
They fly freely and set aflame whatever and whomever they choose
And this time, they chose us
So there we were
Engulfed in a suffocating funnel
Unable to truly see each other through all of the black smoke
Only our demons rose in the darkness
Because when passion unravels itself for the lovers to see
It leaves no stone unturned and no angel unscathed

Mixed Signals

Sometimes I wonder
What intentions lie in between
Your indirect questions
You slip in silent inquiries
In an attempt to mask them
Amid a casual conversation
Except, you do a poor job
Of hiding your thirsting desire
To know and understand me better
But at least, you try

Love Notes

My favorite part of you lies just below your neck, within the protection of your
ribs
My hand loves to rest cradled on your chest
Where I can feel the essence of your existence beating rhythmically
At times I lend an ear to this same place
And listen closely to the beautiful sound
The strength of your pulse
And wonder how it settled on the pace of its song
These moments are little reminders that you are here with me now
And that this is not a dream
-My romance with your heartbeat

Untitled

Sometimes it's the strongest bond that proves to be the weakest link
Even an antique finish turns to dust without routine polishing

The Journey to Solitude

When we first parted ways silence was my greatest fear
It forced me down the halls of our museum of history
I'd walk through the exhibit adorned with moments of our honeymoon phase
And be reminded of the chapters where I fell deeply in love with you
Silence propelled me into an out-of-body experience
I'd watch us gaze into each other's eyes on a Saturday morning...when all lovers have to do is whatever they please
I'd walk through the halls illuminated with moments from our peak phase
We were solid in love, faith in one another and planted firmly in soil that was rich in the foundation of our friendship
At the time, we thought our only option was to sprout
There's no surprise then, what happened next...each and every time I found myself alone, in a silent moment
I was forced to relive our fall from grace
In these halls, I watched us gradually begin to take each other for granted
We began to act entitled with our love rather than grateful
We began to treat our love as a given and a fact as opposed to something that was sacred and something that is to be protected
We began to put our egos before the health of our love
We began to play dangerously with something we once handled so delicately
So you can see then - why I grew to hate silence for some time
It forced me to own up to my part in the heartbreak that took two to make...but requires one to heal on his or her own
Healing from heartbreak forced me to walk these haunted halls alone
It forced me to sit front row and witness all of the opportunities I could have salvaged the friendship, at least
When we first parted ways silence was my greatest fear
Until I took responsibility for my role in my joy *and my pain*
Silence used to feel like loneliness
And now, it feels like solitude.

loneliness: the feeling of sadness that stems from being alone
solitude: the state or situation of being alone
solitude ≠ loneliness

Quit Actin'

I've spent too much time
Writing beautiful rhymes
Attempting to define
How we force each other to read between the lines
Protecting ourselves
Covering our behinds
Me playing it cool
And you acting like you don't already know that you want to be mine

A friend once told me indirect communication is a disservice to all involved
Well then let me be direct with you baby, you've got me enthralled
And it's beyond the superficial and what you can do when I welcome you
between my walls
It's the essence of you and all of what's involved
I'm lowkey tryna evolve
And you're the type of person I want beside me
As I move forward to solve my life's questions, desires and purpose
You're the type of companion that'll make it all worth it
Because I never needed perfect
I've always adored the special quirks beneath the surface

And I'm not saying with certainty that I know that we'll work
But I'd never condone that the fear of getting hurt is worth avoiding the risk to
feel
I mean, that's actually worse
Denying ourselves the opportunity to truly connect
Just to protect our future selves from a fate we haven't explored yet?
Locking the gates to the doors we haven't touched floors of yet?
Grounding our flight before knowing if we can really soar yet?

Nah, I've never been rooted in fear
I don't have a scarcity mindset
I know all things exist in abundance just depends on the seeds that we plant
And since you're already planting seeds in this flower whenever we do meet
And you shower me with forehead kisses whenever we do greet
And you ask about how my day went whenever we do speak
And you try to hide your fascination with me except when we do drink

And your lips they pour truths of admiration and attraction sprinkled with
respect and finished off with satisfaction
So why we acting?

Those liquid courage truths spilleth over once and it ain't no redacting

So I guess what I'm saying is...
Actually it's what I know
I'm ready to leave the play it cool act back there at the doe'
I know this wasn't apart of our little arrangement
We told each other we were looking for fun at the time that our frames met
But if you didn't know this about me let me enlighten you now
My lips can't help but speak the truths that my soul pours out
My wrists can't help but write the words we're afraid to announce
My hips can't help but dance to the energy we've tried to denounce
We've tried so hard to play it logical
Each of our approaches have been methodical
Trust, I've poured many glasses of Pinot Grigio asking myself
How did I end up falling for this negro?

But it's been the most interesting fall
I'm intrigued and at this point, I want to know it all
So quit actin'
You don't have to protect yourself from me baby
I can be everlasting

Secure

Relationships are like tied knots
Trust them to unravel without regular tension + attention

Empowered

I always give you a reason to break your gaze
When you look at me in a way
That feels like you're reading the poems I wrote about you to my face
I crack a joke
Or strike up a conversation
That forces you to break
The spell that falls upon me
Every time you catch my eye
It is tough work, you know
To dismantle your obvious plan
To make me say the truest things to you
But I do the work anyway
Because I cannot afford
To reveal to you
The power in your gaze

Heavenly Rage

You make me want to do things that lovers do
Like not use words, for hours
And instead express ourselves through sight, touch and sound
As if we've forgotten how to use language
Because all language ever did was bury what's real, what's raw
You make me want privileges that lovers have
Like the right to 24-hour access to your frame
So I can climb on top whenever-
and master our rhythm until it's a familiar song
You put me in a heavenly rage
We fight using sight, touch and sound
We make love as if our souls know we have future scores to settle
We give each other no grace, no mercy
Just the way I like
You don't need instructions
You know where it hurts the best and the worst
A competitive lover-
You leave no stone unturned
You make me feel crazy like lovers do
Cause I'm never finished when we're finished
I am in a constant yearning for round after round
The moments I want you the most are...all of the time
I want [you] on repeat
You worship my body like a lover would
And then you set it aflame
And that's dangerous, real, raw

Your Presence is a Currency

"Let's order food in tonight. I just picked up some wine."
- Is my love language

Untitled

Like a flower out of water
Our love
Died a slow, wilting death

-Flowerless

Analog

I'm craving something analog, a connection
A bond that's authentic with fearless imperfections
There's no issue we can't solve
Without reflection, some time for introspection and affection
So tell me what you want and all
Of your desires
I want to feel the flame, untamed, give me fire
I want to feel electric and
Feel alive
I want the real deal honey look me in my eyes
And tell me that you're tired of - the status quo
Swiping, liking, fortifying weak connections that won't grow
You're craving something deeper than - what you see
Going through the motions but you're feeling lost at sea
Steady tryna figure out - what's it gonna be?
Career, relationships, finances, build a family?
A friend once told me love ain't complex
Love is pure
What complicates it is the smoke + mirrors we endure
I'm craving something analog, something real
So come on baby give me something true that I can feel
Cause you know there are no scars
That we can't heal
Let's start off with a long walk at park shoutout to Jill

Only Sometimes

Sometimes when I'm with you I am afraid to blink
One second of flesh before my iris and just like that
The moment is gone
The sweetness of you always escapes me when you depart
It's not that I can't do without you
It's that if I could choose, I wouldn't
When you return to me, my love
It feels like the initial inhale after being submerged underwater
Quenched.
I get this way *sometimes*
I'm needy
I'm dependent
But only *sometimes*
Other days I am independent, selfish with my time and happily cradled within
my solitude
And yet at times, my affection boils over
Feigning to make you feel loved
So that you can make me feel loved
Some days you are a *vessel from which my love flows from me to you and
returns to me*
Love, twice-baked is *even sweeter*
Sometimes I need a special ingredient to complete my love's recipe
Sometimes, that's you
But only *sometimes*

QTNA

"What kind of poems do you write?"
My eyes raised slowly to align with his.
"Love poems, mostly."

B.W.M.

I can't name every scar I've gained in love
I don't always have the language
Sometimes I don't even know they're there until they're *here*
Creating waves between us
I'm a progressive work of art
And a work in progress
I thought I was finished healing from the love that came before you
But I've got work to do
And I need your understanding
And I need your overstanding
And I need our new beginning
It's apart of my healing
Bare with me

Saferoom

Being with you sends me into an extreme sense of nostalgia
As if I am already living in the future
Because I know that the present moment we share is not enough
It's as if my soul cannot wait for the future to miss, missing you
I long for an arrangement where thoughts as sacred as these are safe to share

Like a Rock

I feel solid as fuck with you
Because you meet me where I'm at
And you create the space that allows me to love
Unconditionally

Thank you

Eye to Eye

You make me feel.... seen
Like a single rose amongst the dozens that blush when you lean in to smell it
It blooms a little further, its stem stands a little taller as if it needed you to tell
it
You're worthy...
Of my time
My glance
A chance
To be celebrated

The only eyes that matter

You know how song lyrics
say that the world stops
And a silence falls over the moment
from the power of a gaze?
The gaze.
That still happens to me
Who knew there could be
so much energy in the silence

Inspiration

I wonder what the moment will feel like
When you begin to speculate
How many words on these pages
Are about you…

Thousands.

Onwards

Grasping the idea
That your world
Does not
End and begin
With one person
Is difficult
Until
Beyond your wildest uncertainties
Your world continues
To spin on its axis
And all of a sudden
There's once again
A thirst
For life and all of its gifts
It takes faith
It takes guts

-Rebuilding requires audacity

Possibilities

The thing about intimate love
Is that it's nearly **all risk** *with hope* for reward
Even knowing this,
I am all in

Two Halves

How is it
That your love
Tastes sweeter
On a stormy winter night?
There's something about the chaos
And its inability to disrupt our harmony
Here I lay
Cradled safely within your love
And I am whole

My Prescription

You remind me of my favorite healing foods
Like ginger + sweet berries
You nurture me from within
I am soul-full

Eager

You feel like a new novel
I am feverishly turning the pages
Obsessing over the details
Thirsting to know...

How our story ends

journey to justice

Free

Lately I don't feel so free
Cease the force-fed narratives that are incomplete
I know the skin that adorns me is perfect
Not an invitation to prove to you that I'm worth it
The spiritual being within me gives me purpose
And when you take a Black life our ancestral line reverses it
You see we're more than these bodies
We're light, magic and spirit
And our names are so sacred we demand that you hear it
When we're mourning our kin
Searching for answers within
Tell me what would you do
If this war raged on you?
We know this fight is not physical
It's beyond this dimension
I hope we have your attention
Preparing for our ascension
We know our lineage is blessed
Resilience all in our chest
And when we pipe up our voices
We'll make you regret your choices
This is a fight for our rights
So it's the fight of our lives
And your silence compliant
So you best pick a side
There's not a moment to spare
We feel it all in the air
The systems hatred so blatant
What took y'all so long to care?
The systems hatred so blatant
What took y'all so long to care?
We can't even catch our breath
Before we're forced to see
Another one of our kin pleading
I CAN'T BREATHE!
Why must we defund police?
Cause they're predatory
Turn on the news

I rest my case I know you see the stories
We're no longer in a position to wait for change
When our brothers and our sisters out here getting hanged
I said they're being hanged!
This is present-day!
You expect that kind of evil to just go away
A man was lynched yesterday
And you wonder why we don't feel free?
So I ask you again -
What if this war raged on you, instead of me?
I think you'd rise, I think you'd fight I'd think you'd look for light
And when that tunnel still looks dark I bet you'd give your life
To bringing change and making gains towards equal rights
If not for you then for your youth so that their futures bright
So the next time you're debating whether this is a riot, march or peace walk
Turn off the news, go outdoors and let them streets talk
Don't question what me and mine our doing to demand improvements
The revolution will be told by the revolutionaries
Welcome to the 2020 civil rights movement

20/20

The ancestors spoke to my people from the soil
In the midst of an unprecedented year of illness, confinement, and chaos
When some thought our sight would become hazy and our voices muffled
Our source of strength and resilience ~~Trump~~ed all barriers
It was, after all, the year of clear vision
The time for this nation
To fall to its knees
Is long overdue
The time for this nation
To acknowledge its dark history
Are reparations now **twice owed**
In the midst of these inequitable truths
Our ancestor's voices still prevailed over the confusion
Delivering the instructions innately known to us
Our ears rose to the sounds of a familiar cadence
So calm and confident it felt like a song:

"Rise
Chant their names
Paint their faces on every corner
Demand their lives be remembered
Demand that your life be protected
Retrieve this land from its thieves
And return it to its natives
And once again, show this nation that we have not forgotten that Justice is the
only way forward
And Justice belongs to us."

So we rose
We chanted
We stood our ground
We showed America what they taught us: that rage + destruction is the only
language they understand
Black minds, bodies and spirits once again, reengaged in the taxing fight
against the systemic, mental and physical warfare to protect our rights, health,
and families
When we feel helpless, cornered, hunted, attacked and suffocated
Our ancestors emerge to remind us where we've been and where we must go

P.B.W.

My heart cracks a thousand times
Every moment that I remember
That somewhere right now
The bodies, lives and freedom of Black girls
Are being taken for the sexual appetite, entertainment and submission to sick
men
This is a domestic issue
This is an international issue
This is an US issue until it's a NONissue
Protect Black Women
We are not here to be devoured for your entertainment

False Truths

What kind of self-righteousness
Births the audacity
For you to believe
That my skin, which absorbs sun rays for breakfast
And my hair, which defies Newton's gravitational theory
And my resilience, which I borrow from my ancestors daily
Make me less than?
Ain't it obvious that God spent extra time on me and my people?

I rest my case.

1st World Woman

How grateful am I
To have come into a woman
At a time like this
How grateful am I
To have come into a woman
When I can feel, claim and execute my femininity
Without sacrificing the layers that represent my sexual prowess
How grateful am I
To have come into a woman
At a time like this
How grateful am I
To have come into a woman
Where my prerogative - is truly mine
How grateful am I
To have come into a woman
At a time like this
How grateful am I
To have come into a woman
With the luxury of voice and choice

Sadly, these luxuries still escape many women today
They are robbed from women both domestic and abroad by:
Patriarchy
Racism
Gender Oppression
Hate
Socioeconomic Status
Access
and
Resources

So although I am grateful-
I am starkly aware that there is work to be done

Ain't it crazy

Ain't it crazy
That Black bodies are still running after all these years?
Still attempting to attain:
equitable rights
safe spaces
voices
protection
fluidity
the benefit of the doubt
freedom to be

Ain't it crazy
That Black bodies are still running after all these years?
In an attempt to protect:
our families
our lives
our spaces
our opportunities
our bodies
our children
our women
our men
our organs

Ain't it crazy
That Black bodies are still running after all these years?
from everyone
and sometimes
from ourselves

-hatefromalldirections

potpourri

Images Transcend

When I look out to the world I see images of me
Only morphed and altered to a tolerant degree
I see subtle nods and hints of what they aspire to be
As my morphed image transcends into mainstream
I see my sister, my mother, and my sista-friends too
Every fiber of their unique beauty carbon-copied and labeled "brand new"
I see features once classified as over-sexualized or unbecoming
As the very inspiration for the hike of nip, tuck, and numbing
While I fully support the freedom to pursue your idea of beauty
Out of respect for the sistas once ridiculed for having a little more curve in
their booty Little mo' plump in their lip
Little mo' sass when they dip
Little mo' strength when they switch
Little mo' mane when they grip
Those bountiful kinks and curls
That seems to bear the weight of the world
This is a friendly reminder to all my sistas
That we never missed a beat even before they were with us
You've been and always will be
My perfect image of beauty

Retreat

where can I retreat
+ allow my mood and mind to meet
silence the distractions of the world
turn my irritants to pearls
where can I lay low
recharge + and redirect my flow
assess + protect my energy
reclaim my positivity
how do I disconnect
life's synonymous with the internet
time fails to lapse only seems to speed
steady tryna to counteract its agility
the need accomplish mo'
meanwhile, life is waiting at the doe'
no moment to assess personal growth
so instead I wrote personal oaths:
find your own retreat
allow your mood and mind to meet
silence the distractions of the world
trust your intuition, girl
when you start feeling the heat
know that God's grace always defeats
pull back harbor your inner strength
pray that you'll stay within his grip
and when you do prevail
know that it's because you're built to scale
no longer be afraid to be fail
that comes before your upward trail
+ when ya season turns back sweet
allow ya red wine + lips to meet
stay focused, pray, love, repeat
stay focused, pray, love, repeat

Omnipresent

Despite my efforts to conceal my path
The sun followed me home

Afloat

There will be people in your life
That will call you friend
Who choose to remember you
By your mistakes
Cut those chains
Or they'll sink your ship

Thank God

Thank God
For all of the moments
That I felt I was too right
And too proud
Thank God
For all of the moments
That I was humbled unexpectedly
Thank God
For all of the moments
Where life reminded me
I am one small being in a sea of others
Thank God
For all of the moments
That taught me
The value in other voices
Thank God
For all of the moments
That taught me
I have so much to learn
Thank God
For all of the moments
That were sobering
Thank God
For all of the moments
That taught me
The value of patience
Thank God
For all of the moments
That taught me
The value of compromise
Thank God
For all of the moments
That gave me perspective

I could never have remained
The girl that once was
Thank God
For all of the moments
That made room for the woman that I am becoming
Thank God

Level Talk

I began shedding people from my life
Who could not keep up with my shedding of layers
That no longer belong
You may hold onto the ghost of the old me
But I won't.

A Prayer for a Plan

Dear God,

I will not worry because
I know that you have a plan for me
that is greater than I can imagine
As long as I trust you, stay prayerful
and do my best to love others
I will be blessed in abundance
far beyond my needs
so that I can help myself
and then help others
Thank you, Lord
for your guidance,
strength, lessons, and love
Amen

Improvisation

I am finding space
For the pieces of me
That have jagged ends

I See You

Isn't it funny
To witness someone who was so confident in their bark
Dance backward on their words?
What you said in anger
You meant
I watched in silence as word vomit spilled from your lips
If we were never friends
Why try to patch it up?
Why even mend this bridge?
Why even *do this dance?*

ESLTW

My mama always told me
Silence your ears for a moment
And read what's upon their face
What do their eyes say?
When in doubt
One cannot hide the emotion that lives there
When it matters most
Eyes speak louder than words
And sometimes, the message is cause for alarm.

A Letter to the Challenged

So much of what you're going through now is to prepare you for your ascension
Trust the journey of your evolution
It's rarely a pretty process
Some of the blessings I am receiving today would not have been possible had I had my way exactly 1 year ago
We don't always have the right answers
In the moment, accepting this is tough
When something does not go our way it's extremely easy to feel helpless, misguided and stuck
Trust me...
Through my attempt to hold onto something that was not for me longterm I nearly closed myself off to a chapter of growth, exploration and excitement
So if you're going through a tough time
If you're losing the faith
If you need a word or a sign
This is it.
Trust your process.
Look forward, inward and never over your shoulder and into someone else's journey
Get excited for the unexpected blessings that God has in store for you
Because from my experience...
They're overwhelmingly more exciting than anything you could've written yourself
Lastly, fall in love with your life
It's precious and so are you
Be kind to yourself
Give yourself grace
Then make a decision to not let up
You got this

Chasing the Moon

I hope you cherish the moments where you can finally exhale
And savor the sweetness of your efforts
The moments where your dreams finally feel realized
The moments where you feel most accomplished, most alive
The moments where you slow down your life so that you can *feel it being lived*
I hope you cherish the ability to marinate in the victory of your smallest tasks
completion
The modest wins count too, you know
Don't you *know?*
How many times have you really stopped to savor your triumphs
You deserve to bask in them
So *bask.*
Because for all of the moments you felt like you were chasing the moon
Running after something that felt so abundantly present yet ghostly all at once
Your miles have finally brought you to this space, not by chance but by design
So don't blink, let your iris swell with the beauty that surrounds you
Envelop your spirit in gratitude
This instant will soon escape you
So I hope that you cherish it

A Prayer for Wisdom

Give me the wisdom
To break the mold I've come to call my own
And loosen my stubborn grasp onto the "known"
Give me the wisdom
To weaken my fingers when they're clutched tightly to false truths
Give me the wisdom
To *unlearn*

Tears from the West

This had to be what it felt like when they took Pac
Black man, for his people holding down the block
Born and raised in the West so he got my respect
Never shaded on the city showed the cards in his deck
Only spit player shit but he walked the walk
Pure contrast from the niggas that just talk the talk
LA culture glorified from city to city
But his story held weight his journey far from pretty
His life's work captured his come up and his beautiful mind
Threatened a system unprepared to see Black people shine
So what they do?
Pull up, buss out and close in on his time
Betrayed a born and bred prophet right in front of his eyes
In the midst of his grind
In the midst of his shine
Gunned down in cold blood while fighting on the front lines
His method: work, stack and pass some shit back
Circulate the community dollar, get us back on track
Product of his environment so he ain't take no slack
Reminded us we can have whatever if our grind don't lack
His mission was greater than any beef
Greater than the streets
Greater than a system that don't wanna see us peak
So tell me: How can we explain the loss of a legend?
Who we protecting?
Name a Black community he wasn't affecting
Who we protecting?
Not our leaders, not the Trail Blazers or the brave
Black activists dropping dead across this country this shit insane
You can say Nip's death was just Black on Black
But take a second to weigh out the other facts
Like the way, he was rebuilding Black Wall Street
Yeah, the one they burned down when it was at its peak
Or the way he empowered our young Black men?
The ones reminded daily to play twice as hard to win
Or his living testament to acquire ownership to win these are the lessons they
don't teach in mainstream education
His monumental impact connected us even through our pain

I know I'll never roll down Crenshaw and Slauson the same
Trips to Simply Wholesome been good for the soul but now they'll have a different ring
These LA streets he walked are forever changed by his name
Love my city, could never imagine being bred from another
But we gotta shift the culture and love on our brothers
We gotta seek the help before we seek the wealth
Mental illness is embedded call that epigenetics
Post-trauma from the horror of our history is evident
We'll miss Nip's presence in the city forever
Who knew how close to the heart we'd suffer this loss together
I'm unsettled so I had to put my emotions on paper
His legacy inspires me to keep creating and to never waiver
To trust my gut
Know my power
And follow my truth
I hope you uncover what his legacy inspires in you

Rest in Peace Ermias Joseph Asghedom

NYC

I've fallen in love with the consistent murmur of busyness in the back of every waking moment
The vibrancy of this place energizes me on the hottest of days and the coldest nights
I take walks in awe at the dramatic exit of summer into fall and the timeliness of the leaves and how they know to change form and let go
(We can learn something from the leaves)
The slight gloom welcomes me outdoors overnight it seems...after an abundance of summer and it's scorching sun
How does a place as **beautifully chaotic** as this know to change form at the drop of a pin?
I've resumed my love affair with the seasons
Taking in each one and loving it for what it's worth
Somehow, I've even romanticized the neverending sense of urgency to get to and see and do all the things one must do in their day
There is something special about this state and it's 5 boroughs
And that is why I've come:
To learn
To experience
To write
To absorb
To love
To live
To grow

Not the Me you knew Before

I had to reassess
The rate at which
I give to others
I had to reassess
The rate at which
I make myself available to others
I had to reassess
The rate at which
I give my damns
I had to reassess
The rate at which
Those damns are returned
I had to reassess
The positions that loved ones, friends and acquaintances play in my life
I had to reassess the assets that I bring to the table
That is the sound
Of my price going up

With Care

Self-care is...
Getting 8 hours of sleep
Vanilla bean scented candles
"In a Sentimental Mood" playing on repeat
A glass of Pinot Grigio
Working out to R&B
Journaling on a Sunday morning
An 80 min massage
A long drive with a Jhene Aiko playlist
A day spent swimming/sunbathing
Setting intentions
Prayer
Falling in like
Falling in love
Nurturing friendships
Sharing laughs with siblings
Sharing laughs with self
Traveling somewhere new
90s Black Love movies
More Prayer
Giving into heavy eyelids
A bubble bath + a new book
Missing flights home because life's too short to go back on time
Dancing
Writing poetry

Checked In

I been heads down deep in my bag of introspection
If you didn't notice - we are living through a natural selection
An era where there is no false sense of protection
You're either primed to secure a level up or destined to deflection
No more promises to self I've decided I'm above it
I'm making promises to God cause his love? I'm a product of it
So there's no longer time to question: why, when, or how it can be?
When I know I am chosen and there are things my eyes can see, things my
soul can feel, prophecies I know are real
I deaded all hesitation the moment I grasped the wheel
So I sit back and I pour manifestations over all my creations
Because anything I produce he gave me the power to make it, face it, embrace
it
To my dreams, I commit cause these years are dangerous if not well spent
And I'll be damned if distractions are to my detriment
So I rewrote my routines that old shit had to go
They may have worked for me then, but I'm evolving as I grow
I'm assessing every connection with those I used to know
If the energy don't honor my soul shit, it was nice to know ya
I'm locked in, focused, I got tunnel vision
Sorry in advance if you've never seen a queen that's on her mission
I'm making quick decisions
No longer reminiscing
I need focus, need precision, I call this disciplining
I'm making deep incisions and extracting what won't work
This new clarity is scaring me but I gotta put me first
Yeah, I gotta know me best
So that I can pass this test
These are Darwin's rules; don't blame me when I pass the rest
I'm a life lover, yes it's true
I enjoy the journey
But time's a-wastin', I'ma aging ya girl is in a hurry
Gotta mix this juice I'm stirring
When I put you in a flurry
At the sudden sight of a Queen in her light as she putting that work in
I promise you, I'm the type to only tell you once
I can tell you won't peep game til the 4th quarters done
I'll fuck it up and I'll have some fun

Congratulate you on your good run
Always saucin' never salty - the way it should be done

And it should not surprise you that I'm playing for keeps
I'm planting seeds root deep and collecting blessings as they reap
As I stand on the trees my ancestors prepared for me using the branches as
bridges to get where I gotta be
But here's the key: understanding self is where it starts
Can't get to your destiny if the desire don't come from the heart
So I'm playing my part
Outsmarting the sharks
Moving strategically to get to levels destined for me
I been heads down deep in my bag of introspection
If you didn't notice - we are living through a natural selection
An era where there is no false sense of protection
You're either primed to secure a level up or destined to deflection
So I'm checked in

Source

Sometimes I forget I'm a writer
And I turn to worldly things to try to create understanding
Distractions like: technology, food and other people's opinions
When the only source that can provide me true clarity is the one from within
Sometimes I forget I'm a fighter
And I turn to worldly emotions like helplessness
When the only source that can provide me true clarity is spirit
In the moments where I emerge from feeling powerless
It is my own voice that gives me strength, lucidity and vision
And so, I continue to write
And continue to fight

Sweet Savory Summers

If I measured my life in summers I'd count them in...
Citrus libations
Rooftop soirées
Doses of spontaneity
Superfluous laughter
Energy
Flirtatious exchanges
Soul freeing dance
Time spent with loved ones
Journaling
Canary and tangerine skies
Hand-painted sunsets in the distance
Bikini tan lines
Passport stamps
Much deserved Mexican food
Afternoon brunch with friends
Sleepless, rebellious nights with you
Protective styles
Outdoor workouts
Road trips
More of yes
Less of no
Introspective plane rides
Snoozed alarms
Warm embraces

Evolving

I am long finished
With tearing myself down
For mistakes I've already inked into the chapters of my life
Instead,
I choose to celebrate the past versions of me
While producing the new edition
Which simply could not exist without the first and second drafts
Grateful for life's experiences
They make my story all the more rich

Makings of Me

A Libra/Scorpio cusp woman
Loves balance but is indecisive
Values morals (mine, not yours)
A whole lotta spice
Social butterfly
Overly expressive in a say less world
Big on #energy
Emotional
Optimistic
Lively
Intuitive
Dancing Queen
LA to the core
A comedian
Impulsive (working on it)
Passionate
Loyal
Intentional
Doesn't hold grudges (my happiness > your problem)
Proceed with caution
Handle with care

Handful

Every now and again
I remember
That I have the power to co-create this life with the most high
The exhilaration that ensues afterward
Is inexplicable

Your life
Is in your hands
Yes, you were dealt cards outside of your choosing
And even so,
Your life
Is in your hands

I am excited for what you will build with it

So remember with me briefly that you do have control
Bask in the comfort of possibility
Then pick up the blocks of your choosing
And build

Pages

Within the pages of this book
I've loved
I've been broken by myself and by others
I've healed
I've learned to love again
I've laughed
I've cried of happiness
I've cried of deep sadness
I've tasted losses
I've struggled to carry an abundance of blessings in *gains*
Life is cyclical just as much as it is unpredictable
Within the pages of this book
I am a woman
Who has lived
And oh, the opportunity of life
That is what keeps me going daily

About the Author

Photo by Joe Chea

Tatiana Cole was born and raised in Los Angeles, California. Her introduction to poetry dates back to the 8th grade when she began to experiment after being inspired by her cousin, Juliana. However, after an extended hiatus from writing poems throughout the end of high school and her college career at Howard University, she reconnected with her creative roots in 2017 after realizing that her life experiences gave her so much to say. She finds joy in using her voice to not only capture her own experiences but also to relate to others. Her hope is that readers embrace the vulnerability that they have within, get clear on what happiness means to them, and pursue it as if their life depends on it. That is her wish for her readers: *to find and feel the light.*

Tatiana recently relocated to Brooklyn, New York. She works in technology by day. By night, she writes, burns variations of vanilla-scented candles, socializes with friends, dances in the mirror, works out, indulges in sweets, and prioritizes at least 8 hours of sleep.

www.ingramcontent.com/pod-product-compliance
Lightning Source LLC
Chambersburg PA
CBHW030849090426
42737CB00009B/1159